Fire in the Sky: The

By Charles River Editors

The Hindenburg in flames on May 6, 1937

About Charles River Editors

Charles River Editors provides superior editing and original writing services across the digital publishing industry, with the expertise to create digital content for publishers across a vast range of subject matter. In addition to providing original digital content for third party publishers, we also republish civilization's greatest literary works, bringing them to new generations of readers via ebooks.

Sign up here to receive updates about free books as we publish them, and visit Our Kindle Author Page to browse today's free promotions and our most recently published Kindle titles.

Introduction

The Hindenburg

"It's burst into flames! Get this, Charlie; get this, Charlie! It's fire... and it's crashing! It's crashing terrible! Oh, my! Get out of the way, please! It's burning and bursting into flames and the... and it's falling on the mooring mast. And all the folks agree that this is terrible; this is the worst of the worst catastrophes in the world...its flames... Crashing, oh! Four- or five-hundred feet into the sky and it...it's a terrific crash, ladies and gentlemen. It's smoke, and it's in flames now; and the frame is crashing to the ground, not quite to the mooring mast. Oh, the humanity!" – Herb Morrison's broadcast of the Hindenburg disaster

Societies across the globe are incredibly thankful for all the modern devices and opportunities that have been developed over time, including the cars and planes that have allowed people to travel long distances in short times, but it is often easy to forget that all these advances came with a price. Car accidents and plane crashes leave the headlines almost as quickly as they enter them, in part because they're recognized as the kind of things that occur with technological advances.

That was not the case, however, with the Hindenburg disaster. On May 6, 1937, the famous passenger zeppelin burst into flames while attempting to dock in New Jersey, and the horrific scenes were captured on film and broadcast over the radio. The Hindenburg was carrying nearly 100 people and was still hundreds of feet in the air when it caught fire, so the fact that only 35 people died between the fire and the airship plummeting to the ground was much lower than it could have been. Nonetheless, the fact that the world could see the incredible sight and hear Morrison's notorious broadcast shortly after the disaster immediately heightened its importance, and the Hindenburg's name is still instantly recognizable over 75 years later.

In retrospect, it seems unbelievable that anyone would fly in a zeppelin full of hydrogen, or that an airship so flammable actually had a room for smoking, and though the actual cause of the disaster is still debated, it all but put an end to the widespread use of similar airships for passenger travel. As a result, the disaster helped modernize flying and made it more reliant on airplanes.

Fire in the Sky: The History of the Hindenburg Disaster chronicles the events that led up to one of history's most famous air disasters. Along with pictures of important people, places, and events, you will learn about the Hindenburg like never before, in no time at all.

.

Chapter 1: A Ship of Dreams

Reporters and film crew near the Hindenburg in 1936

"Silver in the sky, but in her pictures grey,
People young do fly her, but images grow old,
A ship of dreams she was, a nightmare she became,
Now she has all gone, and silent in their grave" – Trevor Monk, "The Ship"

Though the Hindenburg's end is well-remembered, the era in which it was built is often overlooked. At the time, Adolf Hitler's German government was pouring millions of dollars into developing new technology. While the world watched with some concern, especially as Germany heavily armed itself again, the West was dealing with the Great Depression and intended to bend over backwards to avoid a repeat of World War I.

As a product of World War I, Hitler had a fascination with airpower, particularly zeppelins, which had been used for what little air warfare took place before airplane technology was improved. With Hitler's rise to power came a rise in funding for perfecting zeppelin technology, and the LZ 129 Hindenburg was the flagship of the Hindenburg class of zeppelin. The class itself was named for Hitler's predecessor and hero, Field Marshal Paul von Hindenburg, who had served as the president of Germany from 1925 to his death in 1934.

The LZ 129 Hindenburg in 1936

Paul von Hindenburg

Developed in Germany during the early 20th century, these airships had rigid metal frames, over which was tightly stretched cotton canvas housing 16 large latex gas bags filled with hydrogen gas. These bags had originally been designed to carry the safer and non-flammable helium, but the United States was the only source for this expensive product and was no longer selling it outside the country. Thus, the German engineers, under pressure from Hitler to get these aircrafts in the air, decided to take their chances with the inexpensive and readily available hydrogen.

The Hindenburg under construction

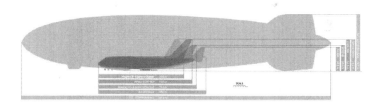

A diagram comparing the size of the Hindenburg to airplanes

The Hindenburg made her maiden voyage in March 1936 by flying around Germany on a propaganda mission to promote Nazi politics, and after that, the airship began making regular transatlantic flights, each of which took about four days. The ship often flew back and forth between Frankfurt, Germany and Rio de Janeiro in Brazil, but beginning in May 1937, a contract was reached that would have the Hindenburg make 10 flights between Germany and the United States. Under the terms of this deal, the owners had made arrangements to ferry passengers across the Atlantic to Lakehurst, New Jersey, from where they would be taken by bus to Newark, and American Airlines would in turn fly them to any other part of the country they needed to reach.

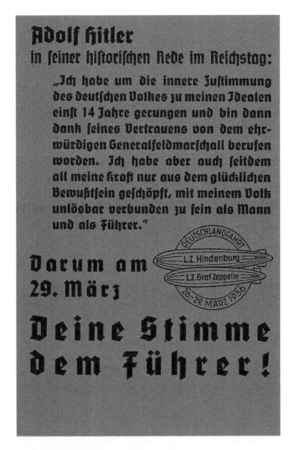

Leaflets dropped by the Hindenburg during its maiden voyage quoted one of Hitler's recent speeches: "I once undertook a 14-year struggle to get the German people to agree with my ideals. Then, thanks to their trust in me, I was summoned by the honorable General Field Marshall [Paul von Hindenburg.] But since then I have directed all my energy to achieving the glorious state of consciousness of being inseparably connected to my people, as man and as Führer."

As planned, the airship left Germany on May 3 and began what proved to be an uneventful trip across the Atlantic. While the Hindenburg was hampered somewhat by strong headwinds, there were no serious problems during the journey, and the 36 passengers on board enjoyed a comfortable flight complete with all the amenities a luxurious airship like the Hindenburg had to offer.

The Hindenburg in 1936

The Hindenburg about to arrive at Lakehurst to May 9, 1936

Among those who sailed on the Hindenburg during its early months in the air were Clarence and Dorothy Hall, and Clarence later described in his diary what it was like to begin a trip on the famous airship: "An atmosphere of suppressed excitement began to pervade the Hotel Frankfurter Hof as the Airship travelers and their friends gathered during the course of the afternoon…Toward six o'clock three large buses ploughed slowly through the crowd which had gathered outside the hotel…The usual passport formalities were begun, tickets issued, and all baggage carefully weighed. Those having more than twenty pounds per person were charged an excess rate. At seven o'clock we suddenly realized that the busses were filling up, so we climbed in and were soon on our way through the beautiful environs of Frankfurt to the Air Field…Before we scarcely realized it, we were up the stairs and within the body of this colossal silver shell. At the top of the stairs a steward relieved us of our cameras, cigarette lighters and matches, the cameras to be returned as soon as we were out of sight of land."

A replica of the Hindenburg's lounge

A replica of the dining room aboard the Hindenburg

It was that combination of luxury and speed that made travelling by dirigible so attractive, for airplanes were still too new to be considered safe by the average person and cruise ships took a week or more to cross the ocean between the United States and Europe. However, the Hindenburg and others like it could make the trip in four days, while her passengers slept in comfortable states rooms, dined in an elegant restaurant, and then retired to a spacious lounge to write letters or chat. Furthermore, thanks to the limited number of passengers they carried, zeppelins were the preferred travel form for the wealthy; with room for only 70 passengers in total, the Hindenburg had no steerage section, and on its fateful trip, the Hindenburg carried only half the normal capacity of passengers, so it felt particularly spacious during that voyage.

In addition to passengers, the Hindenburg also carried a large number of letters and packages on board, usually bound for American hands. Many of those items would be lost in the disaster, and those that survived would become highly prized collectibles among those who specialized in vintage mail.

Partially burned mail that was aboard the Hindenburg on May 6, 1937

A lapel and pin given to passengers on board

Chapter 2: Thinking of Those Souls

"101, a ship that caught your soul, she flew so many years ago,
And in memories nearly forgotten, now all we have is our thoughts,
Thinking of those souls, thinking how they flew their ship,
And how in the end was lost." - Trevor Monk, "The Ship"

On the day of the disaster, there were only 36 passengers aboard the Hindenburg when she went down, and among them were Leonhard Adelt and his wife, Gertrude. She would later describe some of the others on the airship: "There was the old merchant from Hamburg who was finally taking his wife on a trip to America. There was the good, motherly businesswoman from Homburg anxiously counting the hours that separated her from her ailing daughter in Boston. The Swedish journalist with the rosy face was on his way to Washington for an interview with

Secretary of State Hull. The young artist with the gentle, deliberate way of walking was going home to his wife and children on Long Island after a successful European tour. A family from Mexico was enjoying a wonderful conclusion to a visit to their old homeland. American and German merchants traveling on business. Air Force officers enjoying the luxurious amenities of airship travel, having been sent on this trip in recognition of meritorious service."

The "old merchant from Hamburg" was Otto Ernst. He and his wife, Elsa, were thrilled to be onboard, as they had long been fascinated by flight and were looking forward to making their first air voyage across the Atlantic. They were flying purely for pleasure and planned to remain in New York for just a week before returning to Germany on the Hindenburg's flight home. Margaret Mather later described them as "gentle old people who had been flying for 25 years and loved the air." Content in each other's company, they enjoyed sitting quietly by the observation windows and watching the sky go by.

Like the Ernst's, Mather was a fan of flying, but her reasons for making the trip were more practical than romantic. Born in the United States to wealth and privilege, she now lived in Rome but made regular visits to her homeland to see her family. Though she could easily afford to travel on any of the best luxury liners of the day, she once recorded sadly that "lavish comfort and entertainment meant little to a seasick wretch." She spent the hours before her departure touring the German countryside around the airstrip, bidding, as she put it, "a beautiful farewell to earth." Though she felt an odd sense of foreboding about the trip, "I decided that I was tired and let it go at that." Ironically, her foreboding disappeared when she actually boarded the airship and got caught up in the excitement of the takeoff: "It was an indescribable feeling of lightness and buoyancy – A lift and a pull upward, quite unlike the takeoff of an airplane."

While on board, Mather met George Grant, a distant relative of the late President Ulysses S Grant. Unlike Mather and the Ernst's, Grant was flying on business and was on board to study the comfort and amenities offered to the passengers in order to make suggestions to his own company, Wm. H. Muller & Co., for improvements. According to Grant, "From the commencement of the voyage, everything was extremely satisfactory in every particular." His only complaint was with his fellow passengers, whom he felt were "perhaps rather too free and easy" in their attire because many of them failed to dress for dinner and instead showed up in the dining room as if "they were lounging."

Mather also met Herbert O'Laughlin, who was looking forward to getting back to America, where "you can drink plain water and there's no bother about passports." However, she found the closest companionship with John and Emma Pannes, a middle-aged couple with two grown children. Like the Pannes family, Marie Kleemann, whom Gertrude Adelt described as a "motherly businesswoman," also had adult children and was on her way to Massachusetts to care for her daughter, who had recently had a serious operation. Had she not been in such a hurry, she may not have even chosen to fly, although she later recalled, "The trip over the ocean was wonderful. Over Newfoundland, we saw a tremendous number of icebergs, like swimming castles. When we came over Boston Thursday noon, Captain Lehmann said, 'Sorry I can't let you down here.'"

Mather also noticed the Doehner family, whom she learned were traveling from Spain back to their home in Mexico. The father, Hermann, was a banker and was travelling with his wife, Matilde and three of his four children: 14 year old Irene , 10 year old Walter, and 8 year old Werner. These three were the only children on board, and they brought a sense of fun and adventure to the other passengers and crew.

"The Swedish journalist with the rosy face" mentioned by Gertrude Adelt was Birger Brinck, who was indeed Swedish but may not have normally had a "rosy face." It's more likely that his travels in sun that was harsher than that back home had reddened his complexion. Either way, Brinck was often seen in the company of a fellow Swede, Rolf von Heidenstam, and Hans Vinholt, a businessman from Denmark. He may also have met, at least briefly, Joseph Spah, a vaudevillian acrobat and comedian who arrived at the last minute and then spent much of his time taking movie footage of his fellow passengers, including footage of passengers looking at the icebergs around Newfoundland. His film survived and provided the world with one last glimpse of life on the doomed airship.

Karl Clemens also took a number of photos while on board, but he was always under the scrutiny of a member of the crew. Though his luggage had been searched, they wanted to make sure that he was not using any sort of flash bulb in his photography, due to the flammable materials all around him.

Ernst Rudolf Anders, an executive with the first company to produce tea bags, was supposed to be flying with his son, also an executive with the company, but he decided at the last minute that it was too dangerous to have them both in the air together, so he sent his son ahead to America by ship.

Perhaps the most mysterious passenger on board was Edward Douglas, an American rumored to be on the run from the Gestapo because of his relationship with his Jewish secretary. Moritz Feibusch had similar concerns on his mind; though born in the United States, he was a member of a large, extended Jewish family in Germany and was very concerned about the safety of his relatives under Hitler's regime. He had already made arrangements to get many of them out of Germany, but he was still working on emigration plans for others. He was seated throughout the flight with William Leuchtenberg. Since Leuchtenberg was the only other Jew on board, and since the two men were always seated alone, some have speculated that they were the victims of a subtle sort of anti-Semitism, but they also happened to have a number of other things in common, including age and business backgrounds, so it might just as well have been an effort on the part of the stewards to match up two men who would like each other's company.

Other passengers included Peter Belin, an American student, German businessman Erich Knocher, Philip Mangone of New York, Nelson Morris and Clifford Osbun, both from the United States, Otto Reichhold of Vienna, and mail inspector Emil Stockle. As Adelt mentioned, there were also three German Air Force officers on board: Colonel Fritz Erdmann, Major Hans-Hugo Witt and Lieutenant Claus Hinkelbein. They appear to have been given the assignment both as an award and to find out more information about how the airship functioned.

Finally, there was Bert Dolan, who was travelling as a secretary for Nelson Morris, also on board, though not every letter he wrote was related to business. One letter that he carried in the pocket of his suit was addressed to his wife, Mildred, and in it, he wrote, "I know I promised not to fly on this trip, but this was an opportunity I had to take. If anything happens to me, none of us know the Lord's will."

Chapter 3: They Believed They'd Get There

"So much was lost, so many were hurt,
They fought so hard to get their goal,
A ship some said weren't ready,
But they believed they'd get there" - Trevor Monk, "The Ship"

As soon as everyone was safely on board, it was time to take off. According to Clarence Hall, "The men on the ropes paused in their steady march, a few short hoarse commands and suddenly we realized that the ground was falling away beneath us. Steadily we ascended until at a height about 700 feet. Then the distant roar of the motors gave the signal that the journey was actually begun, and into a cloudy sky streaked with red, we glided smoothly upward. In the gathering darkness we could discern the roads and hills. The searchlight in the belly of the Ship illuminated a rapidly moving circle on the ground. In it, one could see the tiny red zeppelin which weighed down the radio antenna-gliding below. Flashes of reflected light from little pools were like huge fireflies in the night far below us. That little red 'Zep' also was sort of a 'cat's whisker' to prevent our getting too low without warning."

Though future generations would always associate the name Hindenburg with disaster, life on board was nothing short of luxurious, and everything possible was done for the passengers' comfort. In describing his August 1936 flight, Hall beamed about the airship: "Inside the appearance of stability and comfort was amazing. Our cabin is five by eight feet, two bunks- one above the other and most comfortable. A stool is the only furniture. A celluloid wash basin, a shelf, a shallow closet and a row of hooks completed the equipment. The walls are of cloth (percale) each cabin a different shade, and the framework of beds, door and stool is aluminum. Painted on the wall beside my berth was a picture of a lighted cigarette with a cross to serve as a constant reminder that the motto of the Airship is, or should be, 'Rauchen Verboten.'"

The amenities around the ship were just as sumptuous. Hall reported, "On the same deck (port side) is the dining salon 25×50 feet. The walls are of cloth, attractively decorated in panels with small paintings in the center of each. The furniture is of metal and red leather. A railing separates the inner space where the tables are placed to form a sort of promenade, from which an excellent view can be had." Since the view from its height was one of its best features, special attention was given to the areas facing outside the airship, a feature that Hall also pointed out: "The windows slope outward and three open, so by leaning out a little, one can look under the Ship or astern to catch a glimpse of the forward motor gondola. The starboard side is the same size…The same arrangement of windows is made on that side."

Then there were the interior features. Hall described the layout: "The deck below is much smaller in area. On it is located the shower baths, the toilets, and a bar adjoining the smoking room. On one side of the smoking room is a low railing. Outside of this, one may look straight down through the horizontal windows. The walls are of leather, gilded on which are designs of famous air ships. Our departure was not to be long delayed. By 8 o'clock we were slipping smoothly and silently through the lee gate of the hangar into an almost breathless night."

George Hirschfeld greatly enjoyed the views offered by the windows, especially early in the trip. He wrote his mother, "We had a wonderful trip in the dark over the Rhine cities, particularly Cologne." He also complimented the ship's architecture, writing, "The airship had a wonderful layout. Everything was very modern, most practical and also roomy. The individual cabins had running cold and warm water. The meals were elegantly served on their fabulous own service and everything was extremely clean. The dining room as well as the lounge for the guests was very roomy and tastefully appointed." However, it was the natural wonders he saw along the trip that impressed him the most: "There were many icebergs and in addition there were entire large strips of loose ice in the sea. The icebergs really looked fantastic. We flew very low over some of them. One of these giants protruded about 250 feet from the water and was 1000 feet long."

While Hirschfeld and the Hall's were enjoying their ship in a relatively sober manner, others, perhaps because of nerves or just a chance to enjoy a few days away from the constraints of home, spent much of their time in the ship's well stocked bar. Mather later wrote of running into Leuchtenberg, "As I leaned out of an open window, I heard short, jerky exclamations of 'Mein Gott! Mein Gott!' and saw near me a red-faced elderly man who had evidently been celebrating his departure with something stronger than Rhine wine, and whose excitement and enthusiasm found vent thus. His emotion was so intense that he seemed quite alone in it, it surrounded him like an aura, and isolated him; but suddenly he became aware of me and cried, 'Herrlich, nicht wahr?' 'I don't speak German,' said I, thinking it more prudent to withdraw, but 'My God! Are you an American?' he cried; 'So am I!' and he threw an enraptured arm about me."

As the accounts suggest, the passengers quickly settled into life aboard the airship, and a number of them took part in a unique tour that was offered by the crew. An earlier participant later described the experience for posterity, and it was certainly one that would not be allowed today for fear of major lawsuits: "Led by one of the engineers, we were led through a vestibule and then a door, and found ourselves upon the 'Cat Walk', really the keel of the Ship. It is a plank about one foot wide extending from tip to tip. The circular ribs of the Ship are bound together by wires and cross members with the walk as sort of a spinal column. Along this path we walked with nothing between us and the ocean far below except the fabric skin of the hull and a few wires and a rope, at which we clutched grimly. Past crews quarters, repair stations, gas and oil tanks, water cisterns and storage sections we crawled. The roar of the motors increased, and beyond and quite unexpectedly, our guide pulled a cord. Like a window shade, the skin of the ship opened and there we were looking down 3,000 feet to the sea."

Chapter 4: Local People Worried

"Flying low, Flying slow, local people worried,
She doesn't look right, she's stretched too much,
A bad omen was what they dreaded" - Trevor Monk, "The Ship"

People have a tendency to look for some sort of sign or bad omen that preceded a disaster and thus could have provided a warning of impending doom. Of course, people often have a bad feeling about things that turn out fine, but with that said, there were a number of problems aboard the airship that converged and probably contributed to the disaster.

The main threat to most forms of transportation is weather, and the Hindenburg had its fair share of bad luck in that area on the way over from Germany. The captain, Max Pruss, confided to a number of passengers that the headwinds had been against them the entire trip across the ocean, and he even admitted that it was some of the worst weather he had flown through. This surprised the passengers, since the ship seemed steady, and certainly much more stable than a ship on the water. The Hindenburg certainly bounced about less than any airplane some of the passengers might have flown on, but the most important result was that the winds delayed the Hindenburg's arrival in Lakehurst by about 8 hours. For that reason, the captain was anxious to make up time.

Of course, there was one small group of passengers who were unconcerned about both the weather and the delays it caused. As soon as they finished lunch on May 6th, the Doehner children scrambled from the table and made their way to the windows, where they stared with excitement as they sailed over New York City and saw the Empire State Building. As is typically the case with families, the parents' anxiety more than made up for what their children were not feeling, and Mrs. Doehner in particular was concerned. She told her husband, "I'll be glad when we're on the ground."

Investigators would later wonder if Captain Pruss took unnecessary chances when he landed, but while it would be easy to point to that and to say that he was being reckless and cost people their lives, there is no evidence to support that. Instead, he simply had to make the best decision he could when faced with yet another weather problem: lightning. Due to the storms in the area, Pruss changed the Hindenburg's approach, exciting many New Yorkers by bringing her in over Manhattan. Men and women stopped working and children ceased playing to run outside and see the giant zeppelin floating almost silently above them, the only sound being that of her puttering steering engines.

When Pruss made his first pass over Lakehurst at around 4:00 p.m., it was still too stormy to land, so he invited passengers to look out the windows and enjoy a tour of New Jersey coastline as he traveled up it to escape the bad weather. Frank Ward was a member of the ground crew that day, and he later recalled his feelings as the mighty zeppelin came in: "And I was staring right up at Captain Pruss, who had his gondola window open and had his elbows on the windowsill, looking out, surveying the situation. And I, my thoughts at that time as I looked up, I thought, we were pulling on the rope, and one chief petty officer from the tower of the 200-foot mooring mast would be yelling orders, 'Bow, pull, starboard'…'Port, port, starboard,' and guiding us and pulling. And I looked up at Captain Pruss, and I thought, 'You know,' my thoughts went back, 'this is not a bad job because the future is still ahead, and perhaps someday the sky will be filled with blimps and air, big 700-800 foot airliners, that will be going from country to country, and that wouldn't be a bad job. I might look into that someday, in a few years…'"

Mather was one of those watching out the window that day. She had felt increasingly better throughout the trip and "awoke in the morning with a feeling of well-being and happiness such as one rarely experiences after youth has passed." She was joined by Belin, who was still busy taking photos, and Emma Pannes, who was excitedly pointing to the town on the coast where she lived. For the next two hours, they traveled up the coast, killing time and thrilling beachcombers below, but at 6:22, Pruss was alerted by radio that the storms around Lakehurst had ended. Still hoping to land during daylight, he turned the ship back and headed for the field at Lakehurst Naval Air Station. Ever concerned about their passenger's comfort, the stewards began to serve sandwiches at 6:30 so that the hungry passengers would not arrive at their destination hungry.

The Hindenburg arrived at Lakehurst by 7:00 but was unable to land because the ground crew needed to haul her down was not yet in place. By this time, many of the passengers were anxiously peering out the windows, hoping to soon be returned to terra firma, and at 7:11, Captain Pruss began applying the brakes and trying to stop the zeppelin over the landing target. However, he was unable to keep the ship steady in the crosswinds, so he had to make another pass over the field. As he did so, he ordered some of the water used as ballast to be dumped so that the stern would be lighter. Those standing on the field to watch the zeppelin land began to pull out their raincoats and umbrellas as a light drizzle began to fall. Some would later claim that it looked like gas was leaking from an upper fin, but that was never verified.

Finally, at 7:21, Pruss ordered the mooring lines dropped. Mather watched with interest as the ground crew picked up the ropes and began tying them to the mooring tackled on the ground, and Belin continued chatting with her as Mrs. Pannes slipped away to get her coat. Meanwhile, the Doehner family and other passengers were watching the landing maneuvers from the dining room windows. Mr. Doehner was filming the action and left his family to go back to their stateroom for another roll of film. The boys were talking and asking questions of a steward, Severin Klein, who was doing his best to keep up with their prattle.

Meanwhile, on the ground, Herbert Morrison was broadcasting the ship's landing live on the radio: "The ship was riding majestically toward us like some great feather. Riding as though it was mighty proud of the place it was playing in the world's aviation. The ship is no doubt bustling with activity as we can see. Orders were shouted to the crew, the passengers are probably lining the windows looking down at the field ahead of them, getting their glimpse of the mooring mast. And these giant flagships standing here, the American airline flagships waiting to rush them to all points in the United States when they get the ship moored. There are a number of important personages on board and no doubt the new commander, Captain Max Pruss, is thrilled too for this, his great moment, the first time he's commanded the Hindenburg. On previous nights he acted as chief officer under Captain Lehmann."

Grant later said, "We were all very gay and shaking hands and promising to see each other again. The steward had served a platter of sandwiches, which we were munching. We were like one big, happy family. Our baggage was all piled up, ready for the customs men. We were laughing and gay, looking forward to landing – and then it happened. In the twinkling of an eye, it happened."

Chapter 5: The Nightmare Started Happening

"Then in the morning at just after two, the nightmare started happening,
As she got buffeted and bashed her nose did start descending, her nose cover torn,
Her gas was gone, her lift was failing fast,
The man at the wheel was fighting hard, keeping her on an even keel" - Trevor Monk, "The Ship"

It was 7:25 when a blue flash caught some of the people's eyes. It may have been an optical illusion or static electricity or perhaps even the nearly mythical St. Elmo's Fire, but whatever it was, it was quickly forgotten as fire broke out from that region and began to spread across the hull of the ship. Morrison was continuing his broadcast as the mooring ropes were secured and was still talking as the Hindenburg caught fire: "It's practically standing still now, they've dropped ropes out of the nose of the ship and it's been taken ahold of down on the field by a number of men. It's starting to rain again, the rain had slacked up a little bit... the back motors of the ship are just holding it, just enough to keep it from... It's burst into flames!"

Clemens, who had gone back to his stateroom to get his suitcase, had just met John Pannes in the hall. He was waiting for Emma to emerge with her coat, but at that moment, there was a flash of light and the ship began to shake all over. Seeing fire engulfing the area, Clemens shouted for Pannes to jump, but Pannes shouted that he must find Emma first and ran toward their stateroom. John and Emma were never seen alive again.

Though an experienced newscaster, even Morrison began to lose his composure, alternating between broadcasting and crying out to those in harm's way: "Get this, Charlie; get this, Charlie! It's fire... and it's crashing! It's crashing terrible! Oh, my! Get out of the way, please! It's burning and bursting into flames and the... and it's falling on the mooring mast. And all the folks agree that this is terrible; this is the worst of the worst catastrophes in the world...its flames... Crashing, oh! Four- or five-hundred feet into the sky and it... it's a terrific crash, ladies and gentlemen. It's smoke, and it's in flames now; and the frame is crashing to the ground, not quite to the mooring mast. Oh, the humanity! And all the passengers screaming around here. I told you; it—I can't even talk to people, their friends are on there! Ah! It's... it... it's a... ah! I... I can't talk, ladies and gentlemen. Honest: it's just laying there, mass of smoking wreckage. Ah! And everybody can hardly breathe and talk and the screaming. I...I...I'm sorry. Honest: I... I can hardly breathe. I... I'm going to step inside, where I cannot see it. Charlie, that's terrible. Ah, ah... I can't. Listen, folks; I...I'm gonna have to stop for a minute because I've lost my voice. This is the worst thing I've ever witnessed."

Looking back on the seconds that it took for the Hindenburg to be completely engulfed, it later became clear that, for most people, location was destiny. Those in the nose of the ship were killed instantly or so badly burned that they lived for only a few hours, and the same was true for those who were in the staterooms or the lower part of the ship. While most of those in other parts of the ship survived, something as simple as one's position in a certain room often determined one's level of injury.

Kleemann had just returned to the dining room from below and was standing near the front of the hall. She would later remember, "I had gone downstairs to my cabin, and a stewardess had helped me change my clothing. Then I went upstairs to the social hall. The stewardess stayed below - and was killed...Everything was so sudden and so confusing. I was sitting next to the window, when it happened, all so suddenly. I was sitting in the social hall, looking out of the windows at the ground close below when two big explosions came. The detonation was schrecklich - horrible. Everything was mixed up. Big men, bigger than John [Bolten, her son-in-law] were thrown against me. Everything was noise and shrieks and screams. I don't remember much of what happened until one of the stewards, who had jumped out at first but then returned, came into the burning [dining] hall and pulled me out."

Mather was also in the dining room with Belin when they heard what sounded like a distant explosion. Belin gave her what she later described as "a look of incredulous consternation" just as someone shouted, "We're on fire!" The room tilted and Mather was thrown against the back wall, along with a number of other people who landed on her. For a brief moment, she felt panic that she might suffocate rather than burn to death, but those who fell on her soon scrambled off and began to look for a way off the burning ship. Catching her breath, Mather remained where she was, paralyzed with fear. Though she instinctively drew her coat up to her face against the heat coming from the fire burning towards her, she just couldn't seem to get to her feet. Instead, she gazed unblinking on what she later described as "a scene from a medieval picture of hell" and waited for what she assumed would be the deadly crash to end her life.

Fortunately for Kleemann and Mather, the flames in the aft part of the ship had weakened its hull and sent both the water tank and the fuel tank to the ground. Without that weight, the ship had enough buoyancy left to allow the portion still intact to settle gently to the ground. Mather later recalled that she didn't even feel a jolt. Instead, she heard voices calling to her, "Come out, lady!" Still in shock, she began a tragically comical search for her purse, looking around for it in the rubble surrounding her until someone cried out, "Aren't you coming?" At that point she came to her senses and allowed herself to be led gently away, along with Kleemann, who had never left her seat and was still clutching her gloves in her hand, though she had lost her glasses.

Not everyone in the dining salon escaped easily. Vinholt was in the rear of the dining room and closer to the flames, so he decided to jump out an observation window. However, he later explained that he ran into a problem: "A woman who was panicking from hysteria tried to go through the same window and for a few seconds we were both stuck there. I managed to get a grip on one of the red hot iron bars on the outside of the airship and that was how I was able to pull myself out. I hung outside for a few seconds before jumping to the ground. I couldn't support myself on my legs, but fell on my hip and laid moaning and half unconscious when three men drew me away from the burning airship."

Chapter 6: She Hit the Ground

"She hit the ground, not that hard,
Quite softly washer landing, but this was going to be a tragedy,
And fire was not long set in, in a matter of minutes,
Her cover was gone, and fire did envelope,
And as men lay confused in their beds, the fire did consume them" – Trevor Monk, "The Ship"

Though less than 30 seconds had passed since the fire started, the ship was now almost completely engulfed in flames. Osbun escaped through a window, but he was later unable to recall how, saying only, "I didn't jump. I know I didn't jump. I didn't know what happened. I can't describe it. I seemed to be dead and alive at the same time." He figured that the window he was sitting in must have given way beneath him and dumped him on the ground, where he and another passenger looked up at the ship, "and as we looked at it, it was burning to cinders." When the rescuers found him moments later, he was about 35 feet from the wreckage and bleeding "as though he'd been punched in the mouth," perhaps because he had bitten his tongue badly.

Leuchtenberg, the man Mather had seen so drunk on the first night of the trip, was also in the dining room and heard the explosion. However, he was able to stay on his feet by clinging tightly to the railing along the wall. Ironically, had he let go and tumbled to the other end of the room with everyone else, he would have fared better, because just as the ship righted itself, fire shot into the room. He later testified that he was "burned up entirely. My face, ears, nose, my lips, everything. My neck was burned, and my hands." Initially numb to his injuries, he looked around the room for his luggage for a few seconds before realizing he had to get out. A crewman grabbed him and asked if he thought he could jump, but Leuchtenberg said he was not able to, adding, "I'm almost all in." Needing to move on to help others, the crewman told him to sit down and slide to the lower end of the room, where Mather, Kleemann and the others were. When asked about his luggage, he replied, "Let that go. I can't take care of it anyway." He was concerned about his false teeth, however, and removed them from his mouth and placed them in his pocket for safekeeping before sliding down to join the others. As he reached the gangway stairs the others had gone down, he was told, "Crawl through here quickly. It's a fire, but it won't burn you."

By this time, the gangway was no longer an option for escape, and Leuchtenberg was told by an American sailor who was helping with the evacuation, "I can't hold you. I'm going to have to drop you." He asked, "How high is it?" The sailor replied, "About ten feet. Somebody else is downstairs to catch you." With that, the sailor called to someone below to catch him and dropped Leuchtenberg into the man's arms. As he was led away from the wreck, Leuchtenberg later recalled, "I was absolutely irresponsible. I was delirious and I could not talk. The only thing I wanted was water."

Morris and Dolan were in the lounge and looking out the forward most windows at the lightning in the distance when they heard the explosion. Morris later compared it to the sound of a service rifle fired from about 20 feet away. As the ship's stern tilted forward, they grabbed the nearest post and held on, hoping not to lose their footing. Realizing the ship was on fire, they quickly made the decision to jump to safety. Morris went first and Dolan immediately followed. As they landed, the burning remains of the ship came crashing down around them, trapping them in a red hot jungle of burning fabric and melting steel. Thinking Dolan was behind him, Morris began fighting his way through the wreckage, not even feeling the burning heat of the steel as he swatted away the glowing hot girders. He later remembered that they were so melted that they broke away "like paper." It was only after he got out that Morris realized Dolan was not with him. Morris tried to go back to look for Dolan but never found him.

In any disaster, natural or otherwise, it is the children's stories that are often the most heartbreaking, and the Hindenburg disaster is no exception. Matilde Doehner was standing in back of the dining salon with her three children when the fire started, and because of their location, they were not tossed to the far safer portion of the room. Instead, as the ship fell to the ground, the fire was already moving quickly toward them. Seeing a man jump from a nearby window, Matilde grabbed her youngest son and threw him out the window to safety. She then grabbed her next older son to do the same with him, but he was heavier and she had to make two tries to get him out. By then his hair and clothes were on fire.

With the boys gone, she turned to get Irene, who at 14 was too big to lift. Grabbing her hysterical daughter, she tried to wrestle her out the window as the flames grew around them. However, the girl kept screaming for her father and pulled away, running back into the room to look for him. With her younger children on the ground, Matilde had seconds to make a decision reminiscent of *Sophie's Choice*. Breathing a prayer for her daughter and husband's safety, she jumped, landing beside her sons and dragging them to safety. The three were soon loaded into one of the limousines that had originally been sent to transport the passengers from the mooring area to their next destination.

Meanwhile, Leonhard and Gertrud Adelt had also escaped from the wreckage but were still in shock. Leonhard later wrote, "Something drew me toward [the wreckage]; I cannot say whether it was the feeling that I must try to save others, or that demon-like urge of self-destruction which drives the moth into the flame. My wife called to me, called more urgently and ran back to me. She spoke persuasively; took me by the hand; led me away." A man soon approached them and led them quickly to a limousine, but when he opened the door, a voice in the luxurious darkness growled, "There's no more room in here!" It was Matilde, holding her two burned sons to her "like a lioness."

Though she did not yet know it, her sons would soon be the only family Matilde had left. Irene was quickly found sitting in shock in another part of the ship, her hair and clothes in flames. Even then, she did not want to jump, but those rescuing her were stronger than her mother and forced her out the window. She was still alive, but she was so badly burned when she arrived at the hospital that a nurse working there fainted at the sight of her. She died later that evening before any of her family members were aware of her fate. Hermann's body was found the next day, identifiable only by the inscription inside his wedding ring.

Of those who survived, few had as horrific a tale to tell as Philip Mangone: "Somehow, in the flashing second of the explosion, I retained my presence of mind. I grabbed a chair and smashed it through the window. I gripped the window sill and looked out. We seemed a little less than 200 feet high. I said to myself, 'I can't jump. We're too high. I'll break my legs.' But I couldn't wait. A moment or two later, as the wrecked ship sank downward, I jumped. The framework of the dirigible pinned me down. I lay flat in the tangle of wreckage, but my body wasn't crushed. I worked frantically to get myself out of the wreckage. Desperately, I scraped a hole into the dirt. Somehow I burrowed myself out like a mole. I was conscious all the time. It seemed like an age before I squirmed through. I stood up, dazed. I wheeled around dizzily. The shock had been so great I didn't know what I was doing. I was navigating without thinking. All around me was the smell of burning flesh. Men were rushing about excitedly. Some were badly burned passengers, others members of the ground crew. The scene was indescribable. Everything was in a panic. Passengers were crying and screaming. I reeled under my own steam toward a building in the distance." Mangone later added, "I was 'alive' for several hours. That is, I knew what I was doing. The burns hadn't got to me yet; I didn't feel them too much. But that night, in the hospital, I was knocked out. I lapsed into unconsciousness. I was in great pain just before my sense deserted me. I was unconscious for a week and after that I was sick for weeks."

Chapter 7: Those Brave Men Who Passed

"But the few that were lucky battled like hell, they fought with all their might,
Battling flame for freedom, and emerging in the darkness of night,
Now so many years have passed, but we all hold a thought,
For those brave men who passed, o many years ago" – Trevor Monk, "The Ship"

Within 60 seconds of the first explosion, the Hindenburg was on the ground and engulfed in flames. Those that would survive the disaster were out, while most of those who would not were already dead. Of the 36 people who died that day, most were lucky enough to be gone almost instantly, killed by the explosion itself. However, those who survived to make it to the hospitals faced slow, agonizing deaths that were most likely hastened by the amount of morphine they were given for their pain. Even 21st century medicine is often impotent in the face of serious burns, and even less care was available in 1937.

Among the civilians who perished, few made it to the hospital. In addition to those already mentioned, Ernst Anders, Birger Brink, Edward Douglas, Colonel Fritz Erdmann, Otto Reichhold and Moritz Feibusch died in the field that day, hopefully instantly. Otto Ernst was also taken to the hospital, along with Elsa, but while she survived, his injuries were much worse and took his life just a few days later. Erich Knocher survived the crash and was even able to walk away and telegram his wife that he had survived, but once he was in the hospital, he took a turn for the worse and died on the morning of May 8th.

In one sense, Captain Pruss went down with his ship by staying on the flaming wreckage until it was close enough to the ground for him and his bridge crew to jump to safety. Though badly burned himself, he returned again and again to the inferno he had once commanded to try to rescue others until he himself was hauled away. Once at the hospital, he remained in grave condition for days and even received the Last Rites of the Catholic Church, but he eventually recovered and went on to give testimony during the investigations into the tragedy.

Most of the victims were members of the crew who were working in the portion of the dirigible that exploded. Among those who died on the job was Albert Holderried, a mechanic stationed at the keel of the ship during the landing in order to add more weight to the nose of the ship. His location means that he either died instantly due to the burning gases he inhaled or was trapped under burning wreckage, hopefully knocked unconscious by the fall.

Captain Ernst Lehmann did not fare as well. Sent on board the Hindenburg by the German government as an observer, he was also badly burned and taken to the hospital. At first, it seemed that he might not be as seriously injured as Pruss was, but he soon began to slip away. His old friend, Commander Charles E. Rosendahl, then in command of the Lakehurst Naval Air Station, later wrote, "As I visited him in the hospital only a few hours before his death, I found in Ernst Lehmann a great example of stoic fortitude; though painfully and fatally injured, his own condition caused him little concern, and he made no complaint. His mind remained crystal clear; indeed, it was Lehmann himself who suggested that he be given oxygen as he felt his strength ebbing. Our conversation was concerned for a time with personal matters; then his mind turned to airships, and I can now see that he probably realized that his life's work was nearing its end."

Among those Pruss rescued was Willy Speck, his Chief Radio Officer, but Speck's injuries took his life just a few days later, in the same hospital treating his captain. Franz Eichelmann, Speck's supervisor, was luckier in that he apparently died immediately, as did Wilhelm Dimmler. Ludwig Felber, Alfred Bernhardt, Erich Spehl and Ernest Huchel were all stationed in the nose of the Hindenburg, the spot of the initial explosion. Felber, though hit with the blast of fire that shot forth during the first explosion, survived for a few hours before dying in the hospital. Spehl was horribly burned but made it to the hospital. Desperate to communicate but not speaking English, he was helped in the last moments of his life to compose a telegram to his girl. Ironically, it contained only two words: "I live." Spehl died before it could even be sent.

Huchel, choosing between the flames and the ground, took his chances by jumping from the dirigible, but he was so high off the ground that he died upon impact. Walter Bahnholzer, Alfred Stöckle, Ludwig Knorr, Richard Müller and Fritz Flackus may or may not have faced similar choices. In the confusion surrounding the emergency, it was never determined exactly how the end came for each of them. Of course, in the eyes of their families, how each man died paled in comparison to the fact that he was dead either way.

Alfred Bernhardt survived the crash and was taken to the hospital, unconscious, in the back of Harry J. Kane's pickup truck. He never woke up and died just a few hours later. A few days later, Kane was cleaning out the back of his truck when he came across a wedding ring. He turned it over to the Zeppelin Company, who later wrote him, "The wedding ring is apparently the property of Alfred Bernhardt, a crew member who died in the disaster. I'm sure that his wife will greatly appreciate the ring, particularly inasmuch as she is expecting a child very soon."

In addition to those stationed at the nose of the craft, a number of crewmen working in the middle of the ship also lost their lives. Ernst Schlapp, Robert Moser, Alois Reisacher and Willy Scheef were most likely trapped on the catwalk running the length of the dirigible when the explosion occurred, so they were most likely killed instantly or trapped in the wreckage. The same was true of Rudy Bialas, Albert Holderried and Josef Schreibmüller, who were trapped within the confines of the engine cars. Of those lost, only Max Scholze was in the public areas; he was tidying up the bar and smoking room in preparation for docking.

Even after the suffering of the victims ended, their families were forced to endured days of uncertainty. While those who made it to the hospital were quickly recognized, the bodies of most of those who never made it out of the wreckage were burned beyond recognition. Those in charge of the gruesome work of identifying them were sometimes able to use a piece of jewelry or a small piece of a personal item to do their jobs. Others bodies, however, had to be held until dental records could arrive, sometimes from as far away as Germany. Only then could a family claim its loved one's remains and move on.

Chapter 8: A Picturesque Delight

A piece of fabric from the ruined zeppelin

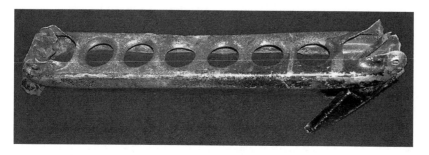

A cross brace from the Hindenburg that was damaged by fire

"A little sleepy village, a picturesque delight,
It could be on a chocolate box, in summer it's a delight,
And if you glance over the fields, you might be quite amazed,
The sheds can be clearly viewed, a homage to airship flight." – Trevor Monk, "The Ship"

Within five minutes, all those who would survive were out of the burning rubble and were either receiving medical attention or wondering around looking for their loves ones. Around the same time, Morrison returned to the air with information for those desperately hoping for some good news. Having gained his composure, he announced, "Well, ladies and gentlemen, I'm back again. I raced down to the burning ship, and just as I walked up to the ship, over climbed those picket lines, I met a man coming out… dazed… dazed, he couldn't find his way. I grabbed ahold of him: it's Philip Mangone. Philip Mangone, M-A-N-G-O-N-E, of New York. Philip Mangone… he's burned terribly in the hands, and he's burned terribly in the face, his eyebrows and… all his hair is burned off, but he's walking and talking, plainly and distinctly, and he told me he jumped! He jumped with other passengers! Now, there's a Mr. Spay, it sounds like Spay, we're not sure of it, and, uh, he also got out, and we noticed the, uh, lines…the different lines, the, uh, airship lines, and the American Airways, their ambulances are down there, and they're taking people out of the wreckage! It seems that a number of them jumped clear when the explosion occurred in the tail. Now, I – I've just been running up with Mr. Mangone, and put him in a car, his wife and daughter met him, and I put them in the car with him, and sent him to the field hospital with the other passengers who have been saved."

Besides Mangone, the other man mentioned was not Mr. Spay but Joseph Spah, whose Hindenburg nightmare was far from over. Not only had he lost his beloved pet dog in the crash, he would also be accused again and again of sabotaging the ship. Spah was a German during a time of increasing concern about Hitler's rise, and he had been seen frequently in the cargo hold (caring for his dog) where many thought the explosion occurred. Though there was never any hard evidence to link him to the explosion, the circumstances led to rumors that stalked him for the rest of his life.

Another man fingered by those who believe the Hindenburg was sabotaged was a worker who died in the blaze. More than one author has put forth the idea that Erich Spehl, a worker who had access to the area where the flames first started, also planted a timed bomb in hopes of destroying the Hindenburg. The theory is that Spehl actually intended not to hurt anyone, but due to all the delays, the bomb went off while the airship was being docked. That said, most investigators and others who have researched the Hindenburg assert that the sabotage accusations are baseless.

Had the Hindenburg burned 10-15 years earlier, chances are that there might have been a more thorough investigation of the cause of the explosion. That is not to say that those looking into the matter did not give it their full attention, but there was so much distrust between the United States, where the incident occurred, and Germany, the ship's home port, that both parties were likely more interested in figuring out how to blame the other for the incident than in finding out the truth. To many Americans, it seemed that the Germans nefariously planned for the Hindenburg to burst into flames on American soil, while many Germans believed that the ship, the pride of the Hinterland, must have been sabotaged by the jealous Americans.

For his part, Captain Pruss maintained to his dying day that his airship must have been the victim of some sort of evil plot, in part because believing otherwise could have called his decisions into question. The company that would have to bear the liability for any loss felt likewise. Those who constructed the Hindenburg and her sisters insisted that only sabotage or human error could be responsible for what happened, since they did not want to shoulder any blame for themselves.

According to a report made by the American Secretary of Commerce about his investigation, there was no evidence of foul play: "After carefully weighing the oral evidence and transcribing to a master diagram the numerous diagrams on which the ground witnesses indicated their first observations of fire, we conclude that the first open flame, produced by the burning of the ship's hydrogen, appeared on the top of the ship forward of the entering edge of the vertical fin over Cells 4 and 5. The first open flame that was seen at that place was followed after a very brief interval by a burst of flaming hydrogen between the equator and the top of the ship. The fire spread in all directions moving progressively forward at high velocity with a succession of mild explosions. As the stern quarter became enveloped, the ship lost buoyancy and cracked at about one-quarter of the distance from the rear end. The forward part assumed a bow-up attitude, the rear appearing to remain level. At the same time the ship was settling to the ground at a moderate rate of descent. Whereas there was a definite detonation after flame was first observed on the ship, we believe that the phenomenon was initially a rapid burning or combustion — not an explosion. From the observations made, it appears that there was a quantity of free hydrogen present in the after part of the ship when the fire originated."

It was that free hydrogen described in the report that would be the smoking gun in the investigation. If there was indeed a leak, and if that leak was purely accidental, then there was less reason to believe that any type of sabotage took place. Of course, the leak could have been manmade, but it would have been difficult for anyone to reach that portion of the ship. Furthermore, the leak itself would have posed no problem had a spark not come along to ignite it.

In the end, it fell to the German High Command to issue a ruling on the cause of the explosion. Put simply, their conclusion was that no conclusion could be drawn: "In spite of thorough questioning of all the witnesses, in spite of a thorough-going inspection and search of the wreckage, and in spite of evaluation of all pictorial documents giving testimony of the sequence of the fire, no completely certain proof can be found for any of the possibilities cited above. In view of the fact that in the German Zeppelin airship traffic in an operation period of decades no accidents have occurred while utilizing hydrogen as lifting gas, and on the basis of all testimony of witnesses and investigations, the commission has gained the conviction, that everything had been done by all parties responsible for the frictionless execution of the airship traffic to forestall an accident. If therefore not any one of the previously-mentioned possibilities of criminal attack can be considered, the Commission can only assume as a cause of the airship fire a cooperation of a number of unfortunate circumstances in a case of force majeure." The committee went on to conclude that the only accidental cause for the explosion was a combination of a leaking hydrogen cell and a spark caused by either by some sort of mild lightning or static electricity.

There were also plenty of other theories, some of which seem more farfetched than others. One author who wrote about the disaster theorized that it was St. Elmo's fire, an unusual phenomenon that can occur when lightning is in the area: "But within the past year, I have located an observer, Professor Mark Heald of Princeton, New Jersey, who undoubtedly saw St. Elmo's Fire flickering along the airship's back a good minute before the fire broke out. Standing outside the main gate to the Naval Air Station, he watched, together with his wife and son, as the Zeppelin approached the mast and dropped her bow lines. A minute thereafter, by Mr. Heald's estimation, he first noticed a dim 'blue flame' flickering along the backbone girder about one-quarter the length abaft the bow to the tail. There was time for him to remark to his wife, 'Oh, heavens, the thing is afire,' for her to reply, 'Where?' and for him to answer, 'Up along the top ridge' – before there was a big burst of flaming hydrogen from a point he estimated to be about one-third the ship's length from the stern." Others have proposed causes as varied as engine failure sparking the flame or even incendiary paint being the substance that started the fire, and people associated with the zeppelin had to dispel the notion that someone may have punctured it with a pistol shot.

The man who used to run the Zeppelin Company, Hugo Eckener, put forth his own belief:

"I believe that the fire was not caused by an electrical spark, but by a static spark. A thunderstorm front had passed before the landing maneuver. However if one observes more closely one can see that this was followed by a smaller storm front. This created conditions suitable for static sparks to occur. I believe spark had ignited gas in the rear of the ship.

It may seem strange that the fire did not occur the moment the landing ropes had touched the ground, because that is when the airship would have been earthed. I believe there is an explanation for this. When the ropes were first dropped they were very dry, and poor conductors. Slowly however they got dampened by the rain that was falling and the charge was slowly equalized. Thus the potential difference between the airship and the overlying air masses would have been sufficient enough to generate static electricity. The Hindenburg would have acted as a giant kite, close to the storm clouds, collecting a static spark.

I am convinced that a leak must have occurred in the upper rear section of the ship. My assumption is confirmed by the remarkable observations by one of the witnesses. He described seeing a peculiar flutter as if gas were rising and escaping. If I were to be asked to explain what had caused this abnormal build-up of gas, I could only make to myself one explanation.

The ship proceeded in a sharp turn during its landing maneuver. This would have generated extremely high tension in the sections close to the stabilizing fins, which are braced by shear wires. I suspect that under such tension one of these wires may have broken and caused a rip in one of the gas cells. The gas then filled up the space between the cell and the outer cover, which is why the airship sank at the rear. This accumulated amount of gas was then ignited by a static spark. This was not lightning but a small static spark, enough to ignite free gas in the rear."

Of course, the same strain of human nature that finds it impossible to accept that an American President could be killed by a lone assassin, or that a jet could suffer massive engine failure over an ocean finds it impossible to accept that 36 people lost their lives to an accident. Nonetheless, blaming a disaster on an accident is usually more accurate than conspiracy theories. Human error happens on a daily basis, and nature often changes the course of history, as in the case of Hurricane Katrina or the eruption of Mount Saint Helens.

No matter the actual cause, the Hindenburg disaster quickly spelled the end of passengers traveling across the Atlantic on zeppelins, despite the fact that such airships had logged more than a million miles safely. At the same time, the fact that technological advances in airplanes made it possible to fly much faster may have made the decline or zeppelins inevitable anyway. Whether the zeppelins would've faded into obscurity with or without the disaster is a question, but some people were still able to put the Hindenburg and its untimely demise into perspective. In showing video footage of the disaster, Britain's Pathe newsreel concluded with these remarks: "The Hindenburg has gone. She represented man's latest attempt to conquer the Atlantic by air. Her tragedy will not halt the march of progress. From her ashes will arise the knowledge, from her fate the lesson, that will lead to a greater and a better means of mastering the air. If so, her dead will not have died in vain."

Picture of a memorial marker commemorating the site of the Hindenburg disaster

Bibliography

Archbold, Rick. *Hindenburg: An Illustrated History*. Toronto: Viking Studio/Madison Press, 1994.

Botting, Douglas. *Dr. Eckener's Dream Machine: The Great Zeppelin and the Dawn of Air Travel*. New York: Henry Holt & Co., 2001.

Deutsche Zeppelin-Reederei. *Airship Voyages Made Easy* (16 page booklet for "Hindenburg" passengers). Friedrichshafen, Germany: Luftschiffbau Zeppelin G.m.b.H., 1937.

Dick, Harold G. and Douglas H. Robinson. *The Golden Age of the Great Passenger Airships Graf Zeppelin & Hindenburg*. Washington, D.C. and London: Smithsonian Institution Press, 1985.

Duggan, John. *LZ 129 "Hindenburg": The Complete Story*. Ickenham, UK: Zeppelin Study Group, 2002.

Hoehling, A.A. *Who Destroyed The Hindenburg?* Boston: Little, Brown and Company, 1962.

Lehmann, Ernst. *Zeppelin: The Story of Lighter-than-air Craft*. London: Longmans, Green and Co., 1937.

Majoor, Mireille. *Inside the Hindenburg*. Boston: Little, Brown and Company, 2000.

Mooney, Michael Macdonald. *The Hindenburg*. New York: Dodd, Mead & Company, 1972.

Toland, John. *The Great Dirigibles: Their Triumphs and Disasters*. Boston: Courier Dover Publications, 1972.

Made in the USA
San Bernardino, CA
30 April 2015